G000089995

MERV HUGHES

BEST SPORTING INSULTS

MERV HUGHES'
BEST SPORTING INSULTS

A collection of killer lines from our favourite Aussie sports

with Daniel Pace

ALLEN&UNWIN

First published in 2010

Allen & Unwin
83 Alexander Street
Crows Nest NSW 2065
Australia
Phone: (61 2) 8425 0100
Fax: (61 2) 9906 2218
Email: info@allenandunwin.com
Web: www.allenandunwin.com

Cataloguing-in-Publication details are available
from the National Library of Australia
www.trove.nla.gov.au

ISBN 978 1 74237 519 9

Internal design by Squirt Creative
Set in 12/16 pt Gill Sans by Squirt Creative
Printed in Australia by Ligare Pty Ltd, Sydney

10 9 8 7 6 5 4 3 2 1

CONTENTS

INTRODUCTION
BY MERV HUGHES

Why is it that whenever the conversation turns to sledging and insults in sport, everyone in the room turns around and looks at me?

I didn't invent sledging and I was certainly not the best at it. Perhaps I was more obvious because I had to do it from the middle of the pitch—seeing as I couldn't be bothered running right to the batsmen's end to deliver my insult *sotto voce*.

Why do we insult our opposition? Psychological advantage at the highest level. Performance is so much tied up in the factors that contribute to a player's 'mental attitude'—and these are especially self-image and confidence—held together by the power of concentration. As a bowler, I used sledging to try to undo one or all of these things in my opponents.

A sportsperson's confidence is based on the ability to perform at the level required to win. Sledging is about finding a real or invented weakness in another's technique or approach in the hope that highlighting it might lead to undermining their confidence. At the highest level of competiton this can mean the difference between winning and not. Although the analysis is elegant, the implementation of a strategy based on undermining confidence can be as unsophisticated as what I once said to Robin Smith after beating him outside off stump three balls in a row: 'You can't f**king bat.' His response was to hit my next delivery for four runs and to reply, 'We make a good pair, Merv. I can't f**king bat and you can't f**king bowl.' This told me three things about Smith: he had a sense of humour; he was confident enough to take me on (so confidence was important to him and so, probably, was pride); and he was thinking about what I had said to him, so if I kept at him, there was a chance I could disrupt his concentration. It took me three days, but eventually I worked out a strategy.

Allan Border told me on a rest day that Smith was planning to stare me down if I sledged him. When play resumed, I was my eloquent self when he ducked under a short ball: 'Weak prick.' Then I turned around and walked back to my mark, with Smith responding with his own choice words. On the next delivery I ran down the pitch and said, 'If you're going to say something, say it to my face, you gutless bastard,' and immediately turned and walked back to my mark. I couldn't crack his confidence, so I attacked his pride. I don't know if it worked, but it amused my teammates.

Attacking an opponent's self image is the less kind, often more clever and often most effective form of sledging. It is essentially personal abuse, based on parentage, ancestry, appearance or individual habits. With all the running up and down, bowlers don't get much time to study our opposition up close. Wicketkeepers and batsmen, who stand around in fielding positions close to the wicket, chatting about wine and recipes while we bowlers do all the work, have plenty of time to do two things: study the opposition batsmen, and polish their lines. So in my day, their insults were more often about physical idiosyncrasies, and they had the luxury of hatching a good line over the often long waits between deliveries. And until the invention of stump microphones, no-one watching knew it was going on!

There is no doubt that the master of the craft in my time was wicket-keeper Ian Healey. Energetic, funny and combative, Heals came up with some crackers. Surprisingly, the best insuler I played against was the erudite England captain, Mike Atherton. He copped plenty from me, and when he wasn't ignoring it, he would respond with a comment that I would often have to think about for three overs, before realising he had insulted me *and* amused me at the same time. In the end, amusement is what insults on the field are about. You might get a laugh from your mates, or you might get a laugh from your opponent. If you're lucky, making your opponent laugh may help break their concentration and cause them to make an error. Either way, sledging will always be part of the game.

SLEDGING 101

BY DANIEL PACE

If courses in the art of sledging were ever introduced into school curriculums, Terry Hill should immediately apply for a job as a teacher. The former Australian and New South Wales Origin rugby league centre was a master in the game of 'mental disintegration', as Steve Waugh once famously described it. Hill boasted an innate ability to get inside the head of his opponents and shatter their confidence. 'Tezza', who played 246 first-grade games, the majority of them for Manly, was the master of getting under a rival's skin. He once did such a superb job of mentally disintegrating Clinton Toopi during an NRL match in 2005 that the New Zealand Warriors centre was hooked by his coach. You could say Hill took him to school.

'I drove him mad for 65 minutes and they took him off the field because he reacted the way I wanted him to react. He just lost it completely,' Hill recalls with more than a hint of fondness. 'He was a good player and he got dragged off, which helped us win the game.'

'I mainly won all my sledges. I had a lot of good running battles with certain people. You can sledge all you like but it's good to be on the right side of the scoreboard at the end of the game.'

Now, students, please listen carefully to your teacher because we're about to enter into the murky world of the ethics of sledging. Mr Hill will guide you through some important rules taken straight from his own etiquette manual:

- ✦ 'It's more about witty sledging where you can put a player off and get a dumb response and then you can play back on that.'
- ✦ 'I believe there are golden rules in sledging. One, it's not racist and two, you don't bring up the other guy's family.'
- ✦ 'You can mention past games where you thought he shit himself or didn't have a go. You just rub them up the wrong way.'
- ✦ 'I've been sledged plenty of times but I enjoy firing it back.'
- ✦ 'You do whatever you think will help your side win.'

Sounds easy, right? I hope you're taking notes. But wait, this lesson is just warming up.

Some opponents will crack under the pressure of sledging, whether subtle or not, while others are better off left alone. The athletes who thrive off sledging feel they have a point to prove and more than likely, fuelled by the fire of personal barbs, they will achieve their goals. Hill brackets former Australian rugby league internationals Laurie Daley, Ricky Stuart and Gorden Tallis in this category.

'It was a waste of time trying to sledge Gorden because you'd just make him angrier and he'd run the ball harder,' Hill says. 'There are some blokes you can't sledge. If they're having a quiet game and they're not getting involved and you start sledging them and they come out and score three tries, then you look like a dickhead.

'If it's part of your make-up, which it was for me, then all well and good, but some guys don't have to do that. I certainly didn't do it every game but I did it most games.'

Thanks for that absorbing lesson, Tezza. Rugby league is definitely a brutal game played by tough men. What about another physical, intense sport but with more emphasis on marking your man and one-on-one contests? Let's look at the AFL.

It should come as no surprise that sledging is rife in Aussie rules. Former Brisbane Lions great and current coach Michael Voss would be one of the first inducted into the AFL Hall of Sledging Fame (or should that be Shame?). Voss was an amazing player but he was certainly no angel. Many of his insults were humorous—you'll find a good example in this book—but they were still insults.

A *Herald Sun* newspaper survey of AFL players in April 2010 identified the code's top five sledgers as: Steven 'Yapper' Milne (St Kilda), Colin Sylvia (Melbourne), Brian Lake (Western Bulldogs), Brendan Fevola (Brisbane) and Bret Thornton (Carlton). Honourable mentions went to: Barry Hall (Western Bulldogs), Chad Cornes (Port Adelaide), Alan Didak (Collingwood), Daniel Kerr (West Coast) and Brock McLean (Carlton).

Geelong's baby-faced backman Andrew Mackie is another who has forged a reputation as a serial sledger. The Cats had flogged North Melbourne by 70 points at Kardinia Park in May 2009 when Mackie decided to rub salt into the Shinboners' deepening wounds. He said within earshot of Kangaroos skipper Adam Simpson: 'They shouldn't give us four points for today's win. They should only give us two because North are that shit.' Charming.

But it's not really fair for the players to have all the fun. Why can't the umpires throw in a few sledges to help spice up a contest? Maybe that's not such a clever idea judging by what happened to umpire Stuart Wenn after a round 21 fixture between Richmond and St Kilda in August 2010. Wenn was caught on microphone telling Daniel Connors, as the Tigers defender tangled with his opponent Andrew McQualter: 'You're batting way out of your league.' The AFL powerbrokers decided that Wenn would be suspended and he was listed as an emergency umpire for the next round of matches. It's a salutary lesson for umpires—save your vocal chords for blowing the whistle and officiating the game.

So we have learnt that you need a thick skin if you want to survive the cut-throat world of elite football. But surely the so-called fairer sex doesn't stoop to the tactic of mental disintegration. Does sledging occur in a sport such as elite netball? Are these tall, gracious women sweeter than honey and loath to become tangled in a slanging match? Or do they bare claws and shoot with their mouths as well as their hands when the heat is applied?

Please welcome into the classroom former Australian captain Vicki Wilson. She reveals that although sledging was rare during her playing days, times have changed since she hung up her netball bib in 1999.

'Players often tell you that there's a bit of trash talking going on,' says Wilson, who coached the Queensland Firebirds from 2006–09. 'It's crept in a bit over the years but it's more just little snide comments rather than trying to chew away at someone and really wear them down. I don't think the game allows for that considering it's so quick.'

Athletes don't always use verbal taunts to try and unnerve an opponent. One of the funniest and most well-publicised examples in Australian sport came from Melbourne Vixens captain Sharelle McMahon, who planted a kiss on the cheek of Adelaide Thunderbirds defender Mo'onia Gerrard during a national netball league clash in April 2008.

'She was up in my face and rather than push her out of the way, I thought I'd give her a kiss on the cheek,' McMahon explains. 'Mo'onia just laughed but it did make her walk to the other side of the court.'

Unfortunately for McMahon, the audacious ploy backfired as Gerrard went on to claim best-on-court honours.

Though there's little time for sledging in netball due to the slick nature of the game, it's a different story in Test cricket where players have up to five days to rip into each other. It's the simple reason why the best sledges in Australian sporting history have been uttered on the cricket field. The pitch can be a lonely place for a batsman when he's under pressure and surrounded by 11 blokes who are relentless in their banter. They have two primary goals that go hand-in-hand: to destroy the batsman's confidence and send him back to the pavilion.

Even the spectators can help plant seeds of doubt in the minds of the opposition. The Barmy Army—a ragtag bunch of English cricket supporters— use humorous chants and songs to sledge their team's rivals. Some examples from the 2005 Ashes series include: 'Get your shit stars off our flag'; 'You're only good at swimming'; and 'He's fat, he's round, he bounces on the ground, Shane Warne, Shane Warne.'

English fans were so ferocious in their sledging of Australian skipper Ricky Ponting during the 2009 Ashes series that England and Wales Cricket Board chairman Giles Clarke took the extraordinary step of pleading with supporters to stop booing him.

A year later, in the lead-up to a tour in England, Ponting told reporters: 'I do enjoy a bit of interaction with the crowds and I think the worst thing you can do as a player is to worry about those things and get upset about them.

'Right through the Ashes it did not worry me one little bit and made me want to try to play well; to … shut a few of them up if you like.'

It's a good attitude from Ponting, who's smart enough to know that if he complains about sledging, it will only get worse. New Zealand's Richard Hadlee learnt that the hard way when he whinged about his treatment from the Aussie crowds during the 1980s. Sir Richard needed to harden up. The sledging was, in a strange kind of way, a backhanded compliment because the all-rounder, who took 431 wickets in 86 Tests, was *that* good.

I'd say you're just about ready to graduate with honours in Sledging 101.

But first let's find out how former Australian cricket captain Steve Waugh used sledging as a weapon to turn defence into attack.

In 1995 Waugh stood up to giant West Indies quick Curtly Ambrose in a fiery encounter credited as a turning point in the series that started Australia's domination of world cricket. Ambrose had repeatedly stared down Waugh during an explosive spell of bowling. An undaunted Waugh fired this missile at the West Indies legend: 'What the f**k are you looking at?'

The towering Ambrose was furious and replied 'Don't cuss me, man.' He wasn't used to being sledged and he clearly didn't like it. Waugh had sent a firm message that he and the Australians were no longer going to be bullied by the Kings of Calypso.

Waugh's surprise sledging of Ambrose was all about being aggressive and digging in against a barrage of brutal deliveries from an intimidating bowler. But the best sledges—and the ones we most remember—are funny and witty. Resorting to racial slurs or denigrating a person's family is cowardly and totally inappropriate in modern society. Respect is the key. If you can throw up some inventive and jocular sledges and still enjoy a beer with your 'victim' after the game, then usually it's pretty harmless.

Whether we like it or not, the competitive nature of sport ensures that sledging is here to stay. At the top of the sporting tree, very little can separate athletes on a physical level in terms of skill, stamina, fitness and technique (champions such as Roger Federer and Tiger Woods are notable exceptions). Often it's mental fortitude that decides the winner of an elite contest and that's where sledging comes into play.

Let's just hope the insults stay within acceptable boundaries and we can all have a good laugh along the way. No need to get personal. And if you do happen to become the target of sledging, remember that the more seriously you take it, the more likely you'll emerge the loser in the verbal war of attrition.

Class dismissed.

CRICKET

~

Fast bowler Dennis Lillee once referred to the arrogant
Yorkshire opening batsman Geoff Boycott as:

**…the only fellow I've met who fell in love
with himself at an early age and has
remained faithful ever since.**

Looks like Oscar Wilde was right when he said: 'To love
oneself is the beginning of a life-long romance.'

~

~

Variously attributed to English cricketers Greg Thomas and Steve Watkin, the following sledge was also used by South African all-rounder Shaun Pollock on Ricky Ponting after his bowling had beaten Ponting's bat on a number of occasions:

It's red, it's round and weighs about five ounces.

Ponting, who hit the next ball out of the ground, jibed:

You know what it looks like, go and find it.

~

~

In June 2009, Shane Warne bagged Paul Collingwood's unimaginative captaincy of England during a Twenty20 world championship in England with the suggestion:

I think he was too busy trying to drive his Aston Martin and fly around in helicopters.

Doesn't sound too bad to me!

~

~

West Indies fearsome paceman Malcolm Marshall
was bowling to Australian batsman David Boon
when he asked:

**Now, David, are you going to get out or
am I going to have to go around the
wicket and kill you?**

~

THE MERV HUGHES FILE

*Here are a few of my more memorable sledges
from over the years...*

Sometimes young cricketers have to learn the
hard way. This particular batsman had played and
missed a thousand times. I couldn't resist.

How about I bowl you a fking piano
you poof, see if you can play that!**

~

~

And it's not just the young, inexperienced ones who need the odd push. English batsman Robin Smith had also played and missed several times during the 1989 Ashes Test at Lord's. I was getting frustrated and observed:

You can't f**king bat, mate.

Smith smacked the next ball to the boundary and replied:

Hey, Merv, we make a fine pair. I can't f**king bat and you can't f**king bowl.

~

~

In the MCG Test against Pakistan in January 1990,
Javed Miandad decided to try to upset me by calling me

a bus driver

every time I bowled to him in both innings. I couldn't get
him out, so I couldn't have a go back. Eventually in the
next Test in Adelaide, in the second innings, I rolled him.
My send off for him:

Tickets, please!

~

~

I was playing against the legendary Viv Richards in a Test in the West Indies. I was sussing him out, not saying a word to Richards but continuing to stare at him after deliveries. Richards became agitated at the silent treatment.

Don't you be staring at me, man. Get back and bowl. This is my island. This is my culture. Don't you be staring at me. You have no right to be staring.

I dismissed Richards with my fifth ball, and decided to teach him a bit about the Aussie character.

In my culture we say 'f**k off.

~

~

English batsman Graeme Hick was being
a bit slow one day, so I told him:

**Mate, if you just turn your bat over, you'll
find the instructions on the other side.**

~

~

And I think I confused England's skipper Michael Atherton
with my sledging, as he once commented:

**I couldn't make out what he was saying, except
that every sledge ended with 'arsewipe'.**

~

~

Once when I was being hit to all parts of the ground by South Africa's skipper Hansie Cronje, I decided to make things more difficult for him. I stopped halfway down the pitch and broke wind, saying:

Let's see you hit that to the boundary!

~

~

Fast bowler Jeff Thomson was a bit put out after missing selection for the 1981 tour of England. He commented:

I've always thought the selectors were a bunch of idiots. All they've done now is confirm it.

At least he was proved right!

~

~

The ever-opinionated Thomson also gave
his two-cents on the English in 1987.

**I dunno. Maybe it's that tally-ho-lads attitude.
You know, 'there'll always be an England',
all that Empire crap they dish out.
But I never could cop Poms.**

~

~

Sledging isn't new. During the infamous Bodyline series in 1932, English captain Douglas Jardine congratulated his fast bowler Harold Larwood, after he hit Australia's captain Bill Woodfull over the heart, with the words:

Well bowled, Harold.

~

~

Also during the Bodyline series the legendary 'Yabba' shouted
this remark from The Hill at the Sydney Cricket Ground,
teasing England's captain for swatting the local wildlife:

**Leave our flies alone, Jardine, they're
the only friends you've got here.**

~

~

Vic Richardson, Australia's vice-captain in the
Bodyline series, responding to Douglas Jardine's
complaint that a slip fielder had sworn at him:

**All right, which one of you bastards
called this bastard a bastard?**

~

~

During an Ashes Test match in the 1960s, legendary
English fast bowler Fred Trueman was fielding close to
the gate from the pavilion. As a new Aussie batsman
wandered on to the pitch, he turned around to
shut the gate behind him. Trueman remarked:

**Don't bother shutting it, son, you
won't be out there long enough.**

~

~

A young batsman once said to Fred Trueman:

That was a very good ball, Fred.

Fred replied, without missing a beat:

Aye, and it was wasted on you.

~

~

English cricketer David Steele commenting to Australian wicketkeeper Rod Marsh during an Ashes Test:

Take a good look at this arse of mine, you'll see plenty of it this summer.

~

~

Poor old Warnie was always being given schtick about his weight. As South African batsman Daryll Cullinan, who was renowned for being Shane Warne's bunny, passed Warne on his way to the wicket, Shane took the opportunity to announce that he had been waiting two years for another chance to humiliate Darryll. Cullinan replied:

Looks like you've spent it eating.

Cullinan again to a beefy Warne during a one-day international in Sydney:

Go and deflate yourself, you balloon.

~

~

England's captain Graham Gooch's comment after
Shane Warne's 'ball of the century' in the first Test
of the 1993 Ashes series, which England's portly
batsman Mike Gatting missed:

**If it had been a cheese roll it would
never have got past him.**

~

~

Shane Warne was famously blamed when Channel Nine's
microphones picked up someone muttering:

Can't bowl, can't throw

about Queensland fast bowler Scott Muller during the
second Test between Australia and Pakistan in 1999.
But cameraman Joe Previtera eventually came forward and
admitted that he, rather than Warne, had criticised Muller.

~

~

South African opener Gary Kirsten revealed how Shane
Warne nicknamed him after an embarrassing incident when
Kirsten tried to chat up a group of women at a trots meeting
in Adelaide in 1994, unaware they were the wives of the
Australian players. Kirsten knew he was in for a ribbing.
The taunts started the next day when Shane Warne,
setting his field, said loudly to Ian Healy:

How are we going to get out Tom Cruise today?

There followed an unrelenting roasting
for the next twenty minutes.

~

~

Australian wicketkeeper Timothy Zoehrer was taking
guard to bat against English spinner Phil Edmonds,
who is married to best-selling author Frances Edmonds,
and thought he would try having a dig at Edmonds'
self-confidence with the comment:

**At least I have an identity. You're only
Frances Edmonds' husband.**

~

~

Former Australian skipper Bob Simpson insulted opener Geoff Boycott, as he strode out to make his debut for England, wearing glasses, at Trent Bridge. Simpson said to fast bowler Graham McKenzie:

Look at this four-eyed f**ker. He can't f**king bat, knock those f**king glasses off him straight away.

~

~

Ian Chappell made the following observation
in the commentary box:

The other advantage England has when Phil Tufnell is bowling, is that he isn't fielding.

~

~

Ian Botham made this comment about Ian Chappell:

Chappell was a coward. He needed a crowd around him before he would say anything. He was sour like milk that had been sitting in the sun for a week.

~

~

Steve Waugh told Ricky Ponting to field close-in after England's skipper Nasser Hussain came to the wicket. Waugh said:

Field at silly point. I want you right under his nose.

Ian Healy chipped in, quick as a flash:

That could be anywhere inside a three-mile radius.

Nasser was out three balls later.

~

~

South Africa's Herschelle Gibbs dropped Aussie skipper
Steve Waugh in a match in the 1999 World Cup.
Waugh commented:

You've just dropped the World Cup, mate.

The Aussie skipper went on to notch up a match-winning
century. Australia then defeated South Africa in the
semi-final before winning the tournament.

~

~

England's captain Michael Vaughan wondered aloud to
his counterpart Ricky Ponting at the start of the 2005
Ashes series, setting the tone for a series where England,
for once, refused to be bullied. Vaughan said:

Who do you think you are, Steve Waugh?

~

~

England's James Ormond, who only ever played two Tests, had just come out to bat on an Ashes tour when he was greeted by Australian batsman Mark Waugh, twin brother of Steve:

Mate, what are you doing out here? There's no way you're good enough to play for England.

Ormond didn't flinch:

Maybe not, but at least I'm the best player in my family.

~

~

In a Sydney grade match Danny Waugh, brother
of Steve and Mark, missed three balls in a row.
The bowler glared at him and said:

Surely you must be adopted.

~

~

Mark Waugh was taking an eternity to take guard, asking the umpire for centre, middle and leg during a Sheffield Shield game between New South Wales and South Australia. Waugh stepped away towards leg side and had another look around the field, before checking centre again. Jamie Siddons, considered one of the best batsmen never to have played a Test for Australia, yelled out at slips:

For Christ's sake, it's not a f**king Test match.

Waugh didn't hesitate:

Of course it isn't—you're here.

~

~

Midway through the Trent Bridge Test in the 1989 Ashes series, English batsman Robin Smith requested a glass of water. Australian captain Allan Border's response went along the lines of:

What do you think this is, a f**king tea party? No, you can't have a f**king glass of water. You can f**king wait like the rest of us.

I guess he wasn't thirsty after that.

~

~

Australian quick Craig McDermott was dismissed
at the WACA in Perth by England's Phil Tufnell during
the 1990–91 Ashes series. McDermott responded with:

**You've got to bat on this [pitch] in a minute,
Tufnell. Hospital food suit you?**

~

~

Sri Lankan captain Arjuna Ranatunga called for a runner on a particularly hot night during a one-dayer in Sydney. Ian Healy responded:

You don't get a runner for being an overweight, unfit, fat c**t!

~

~

English opener Michael Atherton, on his first tour to Australia, was adjudged not out on a caught-behind appeal. Ian Healy commented at the end of the over:

You're a f**king cheat.

Atherton shot back:

When in Rome, dear boy.

~

~

Indian all-rounder Ravi Shastri hit the ball towards 12th man
Mike Whitney and looked for a single. Whitney fired the ball in.

Whitney:

If you leave the crease I'll break your f**king head.

Shastri:

**If you could bat as well as you can talk you
wouldn't be the f**king 12th man.**

~

~

This was English sports journalist Martin Johnson's summation
of Mike Gatting's Ashes touring side in 1986–87:

**There are only three things wrong with the English
team: they can't bat, can't bowl and can't field.**

The only problem was that England went on to bring
home the famous urn, winning the series 2–1.

~

~

South African-born England captain Tony Greig had been fielding close in during the 1977 Centenary Test in Melbourne, and was trying to unsettle young Australian batsman David Hookes, who wasn't responding to the taunts. Greig:

When are your balls going to drop, sonny?

Hookes saw an opening:

I don't know, but at least I'm playing cricket for my own country.

Hookes went on to hit Greig for five consecutive fours.

~

~

An Australian supporter in the crowd during a Test match in Sydney in the 1970s yelled out the following sledge to tall English fast bowler Bob Willis:

Oi, Willis, I didn't know they could stack shit that high!

~

~

Australian quick Brad Williams was bowling to Pakistani
batsman Inzamam ul-Haq during a tour to Australia, and
Inzamam was smashing him all over the park. When Inzamam
hit over slips for a boundary, Williams gave him a gobful.
Inzamam replied:

I thought you'd turn the ball more at that pace.

~

~

Australian paceman Rodney Hogg was bowling to
English all-rounder Ian Botham, who was handling
everything Hogg threw at him. Putting in an extra effort,
Hogg overbalanced after delivering the ball and fell
in front of Botham. Beefy didn't miss a beat.

**I know you think I'm great, Hoggy, but
no need to get down on your knees.**

~

~

A very vocal six-year-old was reported to have
shouted this at a Test match when everyone was
laying into Australian paceman Mitchell Johnson:

Johnson, I've seen roadkill move faster than you!

An impressive sledging debut!

~

~

The group of touring English cricket fans known as the Barmy Army chanted these lines during the 2002–03 Ashes tour of Australia:

**Ball and chain, ball and chain. We came
with passport, you with ball and chain.**

Not wanting to be outdone, locals responded by singing:

**Knick, knack, paddy whack, give a dog a bone.
Barmy Army, f**k off home.**

~

~

Australian vice-captain Michael Clarke flew home to Sydney midway through a tour to New Zealand to sort out personal issues as his relationship with model Lara Bingle crumbled. A Kiwi fan, recalling a controversial Tourism Australia marketing campaign starring Bingle, had this cheeky message put on a banner during a one-day match between New Zealand and Australia at Seddon Park, Hamilton in March, 2010:

Clarkey, where the bloody hell are ya?

~

~

Dennis Lillee made this sledge while bowling to
Mike Gatting at Lilac Hill in Western Australia during
the opening match of the 1994–95 Ashes tour:

**Hell, Gatt, move out of the way.
I can't see the stumps.**

~

~

English first-classer Derek Randall doffed
his cap to Dennis Lillee after taking a
glancing blow to the head, saying:

**No good hitting me there, mate.
Nothing to damage.**

~

~

ICC match referee John Reid made the following comment after Australian quick Mitchell Johnson headbutted Kiwi batsman Scott Styris during a heated one-day match in Napier in March 2010:

Generally the Australian team looks good but there are a handful of idiots who need to be reined in. In my time going around the world, Australia was always the worst at sledging. In fact, I'd consider the Chappell brothers to be its architects back in the 1970s.

I think he meant 'best' rather than 'worst'.

~

~

West Indies skipper Chris Gayle described Australian all-rounder Shane Watson, who petulantly celebrated the dismissal of Gayle in a Test in Perth in December 2009, in this way:

He's so easy to get wound up over silly things. Yeah, he's soft. He only looks big and strong but he's soft.

~

~

Nasser Hussain thought Australian opening batsman
Justin Langer might have been in the wrong job.

**I don't mind this lot chirping at me
but you're just the bus driver.**

Hey, maybe I could have sold tickets!

~

~

South African-born English cricketer Kevin Pietersen made this low blow to Australian all-rounder Shane Watson, who had just been dumped by his girlfriend:

You're just upset because no one loves you anymore.

~

~

Australian skipper Allan Border expressing his
very high opinion of English journalists during
a press conference at Hove in 1993:

**I am not talking to anyone in the British
media ... they are all pr**ks.**

~

~

I must admit they can be hard work sometimes.
Simon Barnes, cricket writer for *The Times*,
had this to say about our boys:

**The traditional dress of the Australian cricketer
is the baggy green cap on the head and the chip
on the shoulder. Both are ritualistically assumed.**

~

~

Ian Botham couldn't help describing
the Old Enemy thus:

**Aussies are big and empty,
just like their country.**

~

~

England's captain Michael Atherton on Glenn McGrath:

A six-foot, blond-haired beach bum bowling at 90mph trying to knock your head off and then telling you you're a feeble-minded tosser ... where's the problem?

No problem that I can see.

~

~

Former Australian opener and Somerset captain
Justin Langer detailed his perceived weakness of England
players in the lead-up to the 2009 Ashes series in
a secret dossier leaked to the press.

**English players rarely believe in themselves.
Many of them stare a lot and chat a lot but this
is very shallow. They will retreat very quickly.**

Langer also described the English as 'lazy' and 'flat'.

~

~

In February 2008 Australian opener Matthew Hayden
branded Indian spinner Harbhajan Singh a

little obnoxious weed

in an interview on Brisbane radio. Hayden was
found guilty of violating Cricket Australia's code
of conduct and issued with a formal reprimand.

~

~

This advertising slogan for an English beer appeared on billboards during Australia's 2009 Ashes campaign:

We're English, We Brew Beer.
You're Australian, You Serve It.

I think we did a fair bit of drinking it too!

~

~

Matthew Hayden once recalled the best sledge
he'd ever heard on the field to respected
cricket writer Robert Craddock:

**I remember once batting just after I released a
cookbook and being in a pretty dark mood after
I got out. Someone yelled out, 'Hey, Hayden!
You're overrated and your chicken casserole
tastes like s**t.' You just had to laugh, really.**

Yes, you do, even though he was right about the casserole!

~

~

This not-so-subtle sledge of Australian off-spinner Nathan Hauritz came from Pakistan's skipper Mohammad Yousuf after his touring team had lost the 2009–10 series 3–0:

We gave 18 wickets to Hauritz—that is more disappointing.

~

~

West Indies skipper Chris Gayle also had a dig at Hauritz during the preceding series against Australia.

At the moment when Hauritz is bowling to me, it's like I'm bowling to myself.

~

~

Shane Warne allegedly said this to Australian cricket coach John Buchanan while pushing a car up a hill, after being called back to Australia from county cricket in England to take part in one of the coach's exhausting boot camps:

I'm as weak as piss, I hate your guts and I want to go home. You're a dickhead.

~

~

Third umpire Simon Taufel uttered these
condescending words during the Test between
Australia and Bangladesh in August 2004:

**Let's hope the Bangladeshis go as
long as their national anthem.**

The Bangladeshi management complained
and Taufel apologised.

~

~

In June 2005, cricketing minnow Bangladesh recorded a stunning upset of world champions Australia in a one-day international in Cardiff. The English press predictably let fly with a barrage of criticism to kickstart the pre-Ashes war of words. A couple of games later, after Australia had beaten England, Glenn McGrath was walking off the field when he approached a group of English players congregating near the players' gate. McGrath cheekily shook his head and said loudly to teammate Adam Gilchrist:

Just imagine losing to the side that lost to Bangladesh.

~

~

A Pakistani bowler foolishly remarked to Australian batsman Justin Langer during the November 1999 Hobart Test:

You wouldn't make our second XI team.

Langer showed him, going on to score 127 runs in a match-winning 238-run partnership with Adam Gilchrist after Australia had slumped to 5–126 in their pursuit of 369 for victory.

~

~

English bowler Angus Fraser once reported in his London newspaper column the best sledge he'd heard. During the 1998–99 Ashes tour to Australia, having dropped a simple catch in a match at Lilac Hill, Fraser heard this purler from a wit in the crowd:

Oi, Fraser. Can we have your brain?
We're building an idiot.

You had to laugh.

~

RUGBY UNION

~

This comment came from Australian captain
George Gregan near the end of their semi-final win over
the All Blacks in the 2003 World Cup as New Zealand
headed for yet another defeat in the tournament:

Four more years, boys.

~

~

English back Austin Healey's comments about Australian lock Justin Harrison won him no friends during the 2001 Lions tour, with Healy spouting insults such as:

My old pal, the plod from the second row.

Healey also contemptuously called Harrison a 'plank'. He must have forgotten 'pleb' and 'plonker'.

~

~

Thoughts of food are never far away from players' minds.
During a Super 14 match in Canberra, Sharks prop Ollie
Le Roux dropped the ball cold while charging to the line
after a tap-penalty in the hope of busting the ACT Brumbies'
defensive line. Brumbies No. 8 Gordon Falcon quipped:

**Hey, Ollie, you wouldn't have dropped that
if it was a Big Mac, would you, bro?**

It took several minutes before the players could pack
the scrum because they were laughing so hard.

~

~

At a Waratahs training session in April 2010, University teammates Luke Burgess and Tom Carter had a spat. Burgess yelled this out to Carter, who was in his club gear:

Hey, Tommy, did someone take your No. 11 jumper?

Carter replied:

Hey, Burgo, did [Wallabies half-back] Will Genia take your No. 9 jumper?

~

~

Queensland Reds five-eighth Quade Cooper commenting
on the Waratahs' less-than-exciting playing in the lead-up to
a Super 14 match between the fierce rivals in March 2009:

**There's no use trying to play their game
plan and play a simple, boring style.**

The Waratahs won the match 15–11.

~

~

New Zealand Herald journalist Chris Rattue made
this comparison after the All Blacks thumped
Australia 33–6 in Wellington in September 2009:

**You'd find more spine at a
worm farm convention.**

~

~

Wallaby David Campese laid into England's rugby
team prior to a Test match in June 2003, saying:

**It's clear that English rugby hasn't moved
on a jot over the past 10 years ... I'm not sure
they know what scoring a try is anymore.**

Two days later England hammered Australia.

~

~

In July 2008, Sonny Bill Williams dropped a bombshell by walking out on NRL club the Bulldogs, with four years left on his contract, to join French rugby side Toulon. *Zoo* editor Paul Merrill made this comment in the lad's magazine's annual 'People We Hate' list:

Sonny Bill is someone who did something no Australian should do, he ditched his teammates and walked out. We're calling him Money Bill Williams for scarpering off to another continent just for the cash.

~

~

The following headline appeared on the back page of Sydney tabloid the *Daily Telegraph* with a photo of England's team saluting their fans after a crushing win over France in the 2003 World Cup semi-final:

Hands up if you think we're boring.

But England had the last laugh, going on to beat Australia in the final, with Jonny Wilkinson booting the winning drop goal.

~

~

Laurie Daley made this friendly dig at the game they play
in heaven at a league vs. union debate in July 2005:

**Rugby league is a simple game played by
simple people. Rugby union is a complex
game played by wankers.**

~

~

Wallaby half-back Sam Cordingley was in a club game for the Brisbane Brothers when a Sunnybank half-back kept yapping put-downs at him. Cordingley turned to the bloke and said:

**There's a reason I don't know your name.
Shut up.**

~

~

This jibe was directed from one onlooker to the
All Blacks fans after New Zealand's 2007 Rugby
World Cup defeat at the hands of France:

Belts and shoelaces, please.

~

~

English rugby ace Lewis Moody gave this explanation in June 2006 of why he turned down the opportunity of sitting out a tour of Australia:

I have been a winner against them three times and there is something special about getting the Wallabies whingeing.

~

~

Matt Giteau was playing against former Brumbies teammate Mark Bartholomeusz (by then playing with the Western Force) in February 2010 when he noticed Bartholomeusz's less-than-lustrous locks. He told journalists:

I'll give him one bit of advice and that's to shave his head, because I think his hair's not looking too attractive but he's playing some good football so that's all that matters.

Ever thought about using conditioner, Mark?

~

~

Wallaby half-back Will Genia delving into the
England–Australia rivalry in the lead-up to
a Test match in Perth in June 2010:

**As a young kid, with the Ashes and the
World Cup, it just becomes a case of you
loving to watch England lose in any sport,
no matter what it is.**

~

~

Waratahs youngster Kurtley Beale expressing his
surprise at the sledging by the crowd during a
Super 14 match in South Africa in 2007:

**I've never heard an Aussie get called a
sheep shagger before—I've heard it now.**

Could have been a lot worse ...

~

~

After trading blows with Queensland Reds winger
Wendell Sailor during a Super 12 match in 2002,
embarrassed Chiefs lock Keith Robinson commented:

It looked like two women fighting.

~

~

Here are some purlers from the traditional pre-match sledging between the New South Wales Waratahs and Queensland Reds. It's all good fun and most of it comes from former players, such as this example from the 2002 Super 12 tournament.

New South Welshman Simon Poidevin:

It was great touring with Queenslanders because it always ensured that there were some terrific banjo players in the team.

~

~

Queensland winger Damian Smith after throwing
a punch and missing the head of New South Wales
winger David Campese in 1996:

I can't believe I missed something that big.

~

~

Toutai Kefu sledging former Queenslander
Brendan Cannon as a 'pie-thrower' for botching
a lineout throw for New South Wales in 2000:

Do those pies come with sauce?

~

~

Queensland stalwart Rod McCall recalling
his experiences of playing New South Wales
during the 1980s and '90s:

**You always knew that in New South Wales
sides there were a lot of big-noting,
pea-hearted impostors.**

~

~

And New South Wales back Morgan Turinui
once waved Reds prop Tama Tuirirangi to
the sin-bin in 2007 with this parting line:

**You're better suited to playing
at 3 pm than at prime time.**

~

RUGBY LEAGUE

~

Sydney Roosters prop Mark O'Meley and Wests Tigers hooker Robbie Farah had the following friendly exchange at the Sydney Football Stadium in June 2008:

O'Meley:

When are you going to start whingeing again about missing out on Origin?

Farah:

At least I'm not a fat has-been.

~

~

New South Wales forward Paul Gallen made his feelings known in the lead-up to the 2008 State of Origin series with:

I hate Queensland times a thousand.

I'm sure the feeling was mutual, Paul.

~

~

Canberra Raiders hooker Steve Walters and long-time
adversary Benny Elias, who had lost his place in the
Australian side to the Queensland rake, became
involved in a fight during a State of Origin match.
Walters turned to Elias and rubbed it in:

**Take it easy on me, Benny. I've got
a Test match to play on Friday.**

~

~

In 2003, Newcastle Knights captain Andrew Johns was alleged to have unleashed a verbal volley on Mark Riddell based on the St George Illawarra hooker's beefy physique. While Riddell was lining up a goal, Johns said:

Are you going to kick it or eat it?

After half-time, Johns continued:

While the other boys had oranges, did you have the buffet?

~

~

St George Illawarra winger Wendell Sailor once spent an entire game calling an opponent 'Kate'. At full-time, the player asked Sailor why he'd kept doing this. In a reference to a movie starring Kate Hudson, Sailor replied:

**Because I'm famous and
you're *almost* famous.**

~

~

Sailor had been sledging Newcastle Knights winger Adam MacDougall after Sailor had scored two tries during an NRL match in April 2009. But then Sailor was forced from the field due to injury and the Knights went on to score three tries—including one to MacDougall—in seven minutes to snatch victory. MacDougall was later asked if he was tempted to return serve on Sailor and replied:

No, I saw him sitting on the bench. I actually thought he might have gone to the kiosk to get a pie. His big backside apparently got cramp.

~

~

Sailor had his pants pulled down during a tackle in a match between St George Illawarra and Penrith in August 2009. After the incident he reported that:

[Penrith forward] Frank Pritchard said to me 'What about the full moon?' I said: 'I don't know about the full moon but what about the eclipse?'

~

~

Adam McDougall opening fire on Sailor
in October 2009:

**Yeah, it's good to see big Wendell Sailor has
lost so much weight. I mean, what's the
big fella down to now ... five chins?**

~

~

In game one of the 2007 State of Origin series with the Blues under the pump, a grinning Queensland centre Justin Hodges held up two fingers at New South Wales hooker Danny Buderus and said:

You're No. 2.

He then pointed to his teammate, and Buderus' opposite, Cameron Smith and held up one finger to say:

He's No. 1.

A rattled Buderus admitted later that week: 'That burns, it burns.'

~

~

Manly centre Terry Hill was renown as one of the biggest sledgers in the NRL. In a match against the New Zealand Warriors in 2005, he harassed Clinton Toopi so much that Warriors coach Tony Kemp ended up replacing him.

I thought you could play … You've got nothing. Where's the big hair? I brought my scissors today so I could cut the hair. You've got nothing.

If it's not food, it's hair.

~

~

In 1997, when playing for the Brisbane Broncos,
motormouth Anthony Mundine pushed his case
for New South Wales Origin selection over
Laurie Daley with these provocative words:

**Laurie Daley is running on old legs.
I've got young legs. It's time for
the new generation, brother.**

~

~

Manly coach Des Hasler made the following offer to touch judges Jeff Younis and Gavin Reynolds, who missed two blatant forward passes during Manly's 18–20 loss against Parramatta in March 2010. Hasler was understandably livid and at the risk of a $10,000 fine for making disparaging remarks about officials, he said:

I'll personally pay for those two touchies to visit OPSM and get a check-up because I didn't know we'd reverted to gridiron.

~

~

Sydney Roosters forward David Shillington
called hooker Michael Ennis:

a dirty little grub

after a qualifying final between the Roosters and the Brisbane
Broncos in September 2008. Known as 'Ennis the Menace',
the nuggety rake was voted the game's biggest sledger in a
2010 *Rugby League Week* poll, with 53 per cent of the vote.

~

~

Wests Tigers hooker Robbie Farah argued midway through 2008 that Ennis had been to so many clubs because teammates didn't like him. He gave him a new nickname:

No-mates Mick.

Farah and Ennis have battled for the New South Wales Origin No. 9 jersey since Danny Buderus left to play in England. Ennis has played for Newcastle, St George Illawarra, Brisbane and the Bulldogs, so I reckon he'd have quite a few mates.

~

~

Australian five-eighth Matthew Johns commented on Manly full-back Matthew Ridge's considerable sledging abilities:

I remember one of the first times I played against Matthew Ridge; I needed earplugs after some of the things he said to me. I felt like going to the corner of the field and curling up in the foetal position.

~

~

A New South Wales supporter yelled this out to Queensland forward Nate Myles during Origin I in Sydney in May 2010:

Nate Myles! Were you at Packer's place yesterday?

The day before the Origin match an unidentified man had pulled down his pants and left a nasty 'calling card' on the doorstep of James Packer's house in Sydney. Myles had missed Origin III in 2009 due to a six-week suspension after he had defecated in the corridor of a New South Wales Central Coast hotel.

~

~

Benny Elias rubbing it in to his old foe Mario Fenech
during a Men of League function in May 2010:

**What happens on an Australian tour stays
on an Australian tour. Oh, that's right,
you were never on an Australian tour.**

~

~

Queensland Origin hooker John Dowling and
New South Wales rake Max Krilich packed down in
a scrum in the early 1980s. Like most hookers from
the old days, Dowling was no oil painting and at close
quarters Krilich was prompted to observe:

Honestly, JD, you could haunt houses for a living.

~

~

Phil Gould wrote these heartfelt words in an open letter
to Ricky Stuart in his *Sun-Herald* column in April 2009:

**To be honest, Ricky, you are the most pig-headed and
ungrateful person I've met in football. I discontinued
my association with you four years ago because
I could no longer tolerate your petulance.**

Why don't you tell us how you really feel, Phil?

~

~

Broncos legend Allan Langer led chants of:

St George can't play

during post-match celebrations after Brisbane defeated the Dragons in the 1993 grand final. The Broncos also denied St George in the 1992 decider. Dragons fans haven't forgotten the sledge.

~

~

The *Chaser* boys hijacked the PA system at Shark Park as the Cronulla players were warming up out on the ground. They were referring to a sex scandal involving Cronulla players and officials in New Zealand during a pre-season tour in 2002.

Attention: all Cronulla league players. Could those people involved in the New Zealand group-sex episode, please report to the match-day office so that you can properly be identified ... and try doing things one at a time for a change.

~

~

Former Test forward Mark Geyer criticising the defence of St George Illawarra five-eighth Jamie Soward after he had missed eight tackles in a game against Melbourne in March 2009:

Unfortunately for the Dragons they've got an Achilles heel in the player who wears the No. 6—his name's Jamie Soward. He's going to be targeted every game … Greg Inglis walked over him like a speed hump.

~

~

Storm player Matt King broke ranks and was
fined $10,000 for this comment on the 2006 NRL
grand final referee Paul Simpkins, made at a fans'
day after Melbourne's 8–15 loss to Brisbane.

As everyone knows, Paul Simpkins is a d**khead.

~

~

The West Tigers' Benji Marshall commenting on teammate Lote Tuqiri's new look on Tuqiri's return to the NRL ranks in 2010:

It's like Wendell's come back with dreads and not that big arse.

~

~

This joke did the rounds after a ruthless Queensland won a record five consecutive State of Origin matches between 2006 and 2010:

The makers of Viagra are thinking of changing the colour to Maroon after research found that nothing in Blue has hardened up in five years!

~

~

After a forensic audit of the Melbourne Storm found the club had exceeded the NRL salary cap by a massive $3.17 million between 2006 and 2010, a series of jokes appeared:

For Sale: Complete Storm supporter's outfit. Shorts, socks, jersey, scarf and flag. Sorry, no cap.

Q: What has 26 legs and can't climb a ladder?
A: The Melbourne Storm.

Q: What's the difference between the Storm and a toothpick?
A: A toothpick has two points.

~

~

The Penrith Panthers' first-ever male cheerleader, Aaron Neich, was out and proud and expecting plenty of heckling in his new role in February 2009, especially from the 'mountain men' in Sydney's west.

If people call me a gay poof, I am and I don't care. If you've got it, flaunt it.

~

~

In March 2008, Gold Coast centre Mat Rogers used
his personal website to describe North Queensland star
Johnathan Thurston as a 'speed bump' in defence, while also
arguing that his Titans teammate Scott Prince was a better
half-back than Thurston. The Cowboys skipper hit back:

**Last time I looked Mat Rogers wasn't noted for
his defence—isn't that why he went to rugby?**

~

AFL

~

Commentator Lou Richards had some great calls for players. Some of his best were:

Built like Tarzan, plays like Jane

and

He's three yards slower than a statue.

~

~

Melbourne full-forward Allen Jakovich always
had a high opinion of Collingwood fans:

**Most supporters are pretty okay but there is
definitely something wrong with Collingwood
supporters. They're just not normal people.**

~

~

Bulldogs veteran Jason Akermanis recalled the first time he was sledged in seniors football, as a 17-year-old playing for Mayne in the QAFL. His opponent said to Jason:

I hear they call you Aker. Is it short for acne?

Akermanis, who unfortunately did have bad acne at the time, put in a shocker that match.

~

~

Brett Voss was lining up to kick for goal for St Kilda.
As he started running in, an opposing player yelled out:

My old man f**ked your mother.

Brett Voss stopped and turned to see who had hurled
the insult only to discover it was his brother,
the Brisbane Lions' captain Michael Voss.

~

~

AFL great Leigh Matthews was commentating on television during a Brisbane–Carlton match, when he made this observation on bad-boy Brendan Fevola:

You wouldn't want him as a son-in-law but you'd pick him in your football team.

~

~

Jason Akermanis fired this shot at former
teammate Michael Voss in May 2009:

**I am hitting 300 [games] at good pace;
I can still match it. You might want to
mention Vossy couldn't make it.**

Voss played 289 games for the Brisbane Lions.

~

~

Hawthorn's president Jeff Kennett had high hopes
in June 2009 after AFL umpires released their
own footy collector cards.

**I'm afraid and fear these cards are going
to be the best non-sellers of the year.**

~

~

American basketball legend Charles Barkley labelled AFL players 'damn idiots' during an interview on US radio in September 2009.

I don't want to insult the Australians (but) I am like, these guys are some damn idiots. Nobody plays football without pads every week for three, four or five months and don't make any money.

At least in the NFL, you are going to kill yourself and … you get to be a millionaire after it's over.

Real men don't need pads, Chuck.

~

~

Austinn Jones made this comment on his former teammate, St Kilda goal sneak and serial pest Stephen Milne:

He's mad, he's officially mad away from the public eye. He'd even sledge members of his own family, probably them more than anyone.

~

~

Kevin Carey had this response to his son
Wayne's book, which contained a devastating
portrayal of Kevin's brutal parenting:

I'll be coming back against all that.
I'm writing a book of me own.
So f**k off.

~

~

Western Bulldogs fan Campbell Paul Davey, 56,
pleaded guilty in court to interfering with player Brendan
Fevola at the Gabba in April 2010. Davey declined
the opportunity to apologise to Fevola, instead claiming
that his actions were a perfectly legitimate trade-off.

**[Fevola] gobbed off at me and I threw some
beer at him, I think that's a fair exchange.
I don't talk to idiots.**

~

~

Richmond AFL midfielder Ben Cousins explained what it was like playing against St Kilda tagger Steven Baker, who was suspended for nine matches after being charged with four offences (three for striking) in a match against Geelong in June 2010:

If it happened at a pub you'd just smash a glass over his head.

~

~

Sydney Swans star Dale Lewis retired in September 2001.
Asked by a newspaper what was the best sledge he had heard
on a footy field, he said it came from an umpire in 1990.

**Stevie Wright was giving lip and the umpire
said 'just shut the f**k up, Stevie'. I'd never
heard an umpire swear before.**

~

SOCCER

~

In June 2008 singer Brian McFadden, the partner of
Aussie glamour performer Delta Goodrem, ran on to the
field for Sydney FC in a trial game to promote his new
soccer-based reality TV series. But the Irishman didn't count
on being sledged mercilessly by the crowd, who sang:

**You're just a fat Ronan Keating …
just a poor Robbie Williams.**

~

~

Adelaide United's coach, Aurelio Vidmar, blamed club politics for a 0–6 aggregate defeat to Melbourne in the A-League major semi-final in February 2009. Vidmar was fined $2000 for this stunning outburst:

Because of a piss-ant town, this club will never win anything until you get rid of that crap.

~

~

Oasis guitarist Noel Gallagher launched this extraordinary, unprovoked attack on Aussie star Tim Cahill in October 2006:

I don't know, there is something about him. I would love to kick him right in the bollocks. He has just got one of those faces. Don't you find his face really slappable? I can assure you, lots of people in England do.

You're no oil painting either, Noel.

~

~

Gallagher also put the boot into Australian soccer in general after the 2006 World Cup in Germany:

Stick to the Aussie rules and the tennis and the cricket and the rugby; you are good at that. Football is the game of the intelligentsia and you are shit at it. You will never win anything so give it up. What do they call them, the Socceroos? Do me a f**king favour, you could come up with a better nickname than that.

~

~

Outspoken TV commentator Craig Foster was highly critical of Sydney FC coach Terry Butcher before the Englishman had even set foot in Australia. Foster said he didn't like the English style of play. Butcher returned the serve in an open letter to the *Sydney Morning Herald* in October 2006.

The *Oxford Dictionary* states that an opinion is 'a personal view not necessarily based on fact or knowledge'. I think this explanation sums up your entire input to the game in general.

~

~

Socceroo Harry Kewell gave referee Markus Merk this
frank character assessment after the Australia–Brazil
game at the 2006 World Cup in Munich:

You are a f**king shit.

~

~

Kewell also vented his frustration after being given
a red card by Italian referee Roberto Rosetti for a
goal-line handball in the 2010 World Cup game
against Ghana which ended in a 1–1 draw.

**I am gutted. The guy has killed my World
Cup. He is the referee; he's the judge, jury and
executioner. Unless I detach my arm and put
it somewhere else, there's no other way
I can move my arm [out of the way].**

~

~

Former Socceroos coach Les Scheinflug was understandably devastated on Australia's 4–0 World Cup drubbing at the hands of Germany in Durban, South Africa in June 2010.

It has broken my heart. What we saw out there against the Germans was not Australian. It is not the way we play the game. We have gone backwards. And I totally blame [coach] Pim Verbeek. He picked the wrong team. He had no intention of attacking. We had no tactics. We had nothing.

The result ultimately killed Australia's chances of advancing to the round of 16.

~

TENNIS

~

Australian Rachel McQuillan had this to say to Pam Shriver,
then 31 years old, after the American had beaten her at
the DFS Classic in Edgbaston in June 1994:

You're old. You're haggard. And you ought to retire.

And they say that women are the fairer sex!

~

~

Russian Yevgeny Kafelnikov was highly critical of the grass court used for the Davis Cup semi-final against Australia in 1999 in Brisbane, calling it a 'potato field' after the host nation led 2–0 in the tie. Pat Rafter's response:

I don't care what he thinks, we're the ones leading 2–0. He can go home crying if he likes.

~

~

Fred Perry was the last British man to win the Australian Open, way back in 1934. But he wasn't amused about the reaction he received from the parochial crowd during the final against Australia's Jack Crawford. The fans applauded every time Perry made a mistake and after Crawford netted a forehand in the final game, Perry asked:

Why don't you applaud that one?

This caused a furore that prompted Perry to ask the umpire:

Is this a cricket or a tennis match?

~

~

Wimbledon champion Pat Cash shared his not-very-high
opinion of Australia's big-serving under-achiever
Mark Philippoussis when he said:

**I regard [Philippoussis] as the most blatant
waster of talent in the current game of tennis.
He is a sulker who likes to blame everyone but
himself for his deficiencies and failures.**

~

~

Cash then lamented the 'over-coaching' of up-and-coming Australian tennis players, on the ABC's *Four Corners* program in March 2010.

They've just absolutely messed up a bunch of really talented kids and we've lost an era of tennis players, unfortunately.

~

~

Cash also caused a storm with an unsubtle claim that several leading women's players were unfit and overweight. He told a London newspaper in January 2001:

When you look at her [Lindsay Davenport], you think, 'Whoah, there is no way she is going to be a tennis player—put her in the shot put instead.'

~

THE LLEYTON HEWITT FILE

No other athlete in Australia polarises opinion like Lleyton Hewitt. Some people adore him for his grit, tenacity and never-say-die attitude, which enabled him to become world No.1 at age 20 in November 2001. But others see him as petulant, arrogant and find his 'come on' catchcry annoying. Here's a collection of his remarks which have landed the feisty South Australian in hot water.

~

JANUARY 2000: A teenage Hewitt, upset after his hometown crowd raucously cheered on his unheralded Aussie opponent, Dejan Petrovic, during a tournament in Adelaide, slammed

the stupidity of the Australian public

at a press conference. A month later, *Inside Sport* magazine rated him as Australia's least-admired sportsperson.

~

~

MAY 2001: Hewitt was fined US$1000
for calling chair umpire Andres Egli

a spastic

during a French Open fourth-round match. Hewitt
apologised, but declined an invitation from the Spastic
Centre of Australia to visit one of its centres.

~

~

SEPTEMBER 2001: Hewitt was accused of racism during a match against African-American opponent James Blake at the US Open. Upset at twice being foot-faulted, Hewitt approached the umpire demanding the linesman in question—also an African-American—be changed. Hewitt said, gesturing first at Blake and then at the linesman:

Look at him and you tell me what the similarity is.

Hewitt insisted there were no racial overtones in his outburst, escaped punishment and won the tournament, beating Pete Sampras in the final.

~

~

JANUARY 2005: During a spiteful Davis Cup tie between Australia and New Zealand, Argentinean newspaper *La Nacion* listed Hewitt as the country's fifth most-hated sportsman. Argentine player Guillermo Coria said:

You really feel like killing him. As a person, I would rather not win a single tournament in my life than be like him.

~

~

JUNE 2009: Hewitt brought controversy to Wimbledon by suggesting females should not play five-set matches because they didn't possess sufficient fitness levels.

There would obviously be question marks [over whether] a lot of them could last that much.

~

~

JANUARY 2010: Hewitt had dismissed the Davis Cup claims of teenager Bernard Tomic in January 2010 in the lead-up to Australia's tie against Taiwan in Melbourne and the Tomic camp was not impressed. Bernard's father, John Tomic, hit back.

I think Lleyton had lots of wine during the new year.

Hewitt was enraged in June 2009 when Bernard Tomic ignored his invitation to practise with him at Wimbledon, sparking a bitter feud between the pair.

~

GOLF

~

Australia's Stuart Appleby argued that American
golfers left half their talent at customs.

**They're like a bag of prawns on a hot
Sunday. They don't travel well.**

~

~

Wayne Grady was unhappy with the super-slick 12th green at Moonah Links, which had to be watered to slow it down, during the first round of the Australian Open in November 2005. So he yelled to Colin Phillips, the retiring Australian Open chief organiser:

Well done, Colin, you are in charge of another f**k-up at the Australian Open. Don't let the door hit you on the arse on the way out.

~

~

Wayne Grady had this to say about NBC Sports golf commentator Johnny Miller's supposed bias against Australian golfers in August 2006:

Johnny Miller is paid a fortune because of who he is, but he is a f**king dickhead, and you can quote that. He proved that a couple of years ago when he said Craig Parry had a swing which would make Ben Hogan puke.

~

~

Little-known Melbourne pro Ben Bunny rocked up
to the practice range at Carnoustie, Scotland, in
preparation for the 2007 British Open. American
Fred Funk spotted Bunny, walked over and said:

**I just want to say thanks very much for
relieving me of the silliest name in golf.**

~

BOXING

~

Australia's triple world champion Jeff Fenech has been
a harsh critic of Anthony Mundine, who quit rugby league
in 2000 to take up boxing. In October 2007 Mundine
responded to the Fenech barbs:

**I'm just sick of [Fenech] always having a go at me.
It's been going on since day one that I came to
boxing. To me that's jealousy and envy.**

~

~

Before fighting against reigning IBF super middleweight champion Sven Ottke in January 2001, Mundine made this claim:

Ottke hits like a woman.

A woman with a good right hook! Mundine was knocked unconscious in round 10.

~

~

Mundine again, before his fight with
Guy Waters in October 2001:

**I'm in kill mode ... I'm in the frame of mind
where if I could kill him in the ring I would.
Come tomorrow night you better have
a coffin ready for him.**

This time, Mundine knocked out
Waters in the second round.

~

THE MUNDINE VS. GREEN FILE

Australian boxers Anthony Mundine and Danny Green have fought a running battle over the years to decide who can lay crown to being the best in the country. There's no love lost between these pugilists.

MARCH 2002: After Mundine beat Brad Mayo on points in Townsville, he called Green a bum in a live television interview.

MAY 2006: The pair clashed in a sell-out fight in Perth, with Mundine outclassing Green over the full distance.

~

~

DECEMBER 2009: After Green beat legendary fighter Roy Jones Jr, he said this about Mundine:

The guy's a piss ant. He is busy taking on chumps and taking on babies while I am defeating the best in the world.

In the same month, Mundine hit back:

He [Green] ain't even a great notch on my record. I tattooed him. But throw some numbers at me and I'll gladly whip that arse again.

~

~

FEBRUARY 2010: Green labelled Mundine
a 'coward' and a 'fraud' for refusing his latest
offer of a re-match between them.

**If Anthony Mundine doesn't take this fight,
he should find another country to live in and
hang his head in shame. It would show his
true colours, he is weak, he is a fraud.**

~

~

APRIL 2010: Green promised to 'monster'
Mundine as he again called for a re-match.

**I'll monster him into retirement and
he knows that, hence the reason he
doesn't want to fight.**

~

BEST OF
THE REST

MOTOR RACING

~

V8 Supercars veteran Russell Ingall made this
comment on James Courtney, who enjoyed himself
a bit too much when he appeared on the TV series
Dancing with the Stars in 2007:

**He's a pretty boy who ... seems to like the
Hollywood stuff more than the racing.**

~

~

V8 Supercars driver Ricky Kelly bagged
Courtney in June 2009:

**I don't know how he can lie straight in his
solarium when all his crew guys seem to do
is pull all-nighters to repair his race cars.**

At least he had a nice tan!

~

~

In July 2010 Todd Kelly also had a crack at Courtney. Rivals had accused Courtney of ignoring a V8 Supercars drivers' agreement, by breaking formation during practice and before qualifying by passing cars in order to gain track position.

From my point of view, the guy is being a pussy. It's a gentleman's agreement but he's not a gentleman. That's where the problem starts. Maybe we should have a muppets' agreement.

~

NETBALL

~

Australian netball captain Liz Ellis gave a bit of schtick to the Kiwis about their accent in 2005.

When we go to New Zealand, I just want to say, like, can't you just buy a vowel for 50 bucks?

The response from New Zealand Press Association columnist Greg Tourelle on behalf of the reigning world champions was even better.

Now listen, Leez, there are four vowels in world champions—that'll be 200 bucks, thanks.

~

SWIMMING

~

This was American star Gary Hall Jr's infamous quip directed towards Australia's 4x100m freestyle relay team before the 2000 Sydney Olympics:

We'll smash them like guitars.

Hall was forced to eat his words after the Aussies, led by a young Ian Thorpe, beat their more fancied American rivals to win the gold medal.

~